Acknowledgements

The writing of this Short History was only made possible by the kindness and help given by past and present members of the Potterspury and Yardley Gobion United Reformed Church who also supplied some of the photographs and gave permission for their inclusion in this work.

The Church Meeting Minute Books and Registers and other documents, now deposited at the Northamptonshire Record Office, have provided much of the research material. Thank you to the staff at the Record Office for their help and advice.

Information was also obtained from Dr Williams' Library, London and The United Reformed Church Archives, London. Sincere thanks also to Ron Greenhall, who was a guiding spirit in the early days of my research, for his most helpful suggestions regarding the lay-out and content of my history.

Thank you too to all my many friends and relations for their help and encouragement.

Jack Clamp

Jack Clamp was born in New Bradwell, Bucks in 1928. After a period as an instrument maker and service in the Royal Signals as a radio mechanic, he became a teacher in 1959 at what is now known as the Radcliffe School, Wolverton. Whilst there he obtained a Diploma in Education from London University and in 1971 was appointed Deputy Headteacher at the County Primary School, Potterspury, Northamptonshire. He became Headteacher in 1974 and remained there until his retirement in 1988.

He has for many years been interested in History and particularly Local History and has published several books and articles on the subject such as *A School for Potterspury* an account of the foundation of the school in 1817 until the late nineteen-eighties published in 1989.

In 1992 a Transcription with Additional Information and Comments of *A Brief Narrative of the Rise and Progress of the Independany Church at Potterspury* by James Slye was also published.

An article published in the Northamptonshire Record Society Past and Present 1992-93 magazine entitled *Potterspury's Clerical Mathematician* eventually resulted in the Potterspury Primary School being renamed as The John Hellns Primary School, in 1990.

One unpublished work was *The First Twenty-Five Years of an Orchestra, 1971-1996* which chronicled the birth and early life of the Milton Keynes Sinfonia. He was a founder member of this amateur orchestra.

His latest publication, *An Illustrated History of The Protestant Dissenting Church Potterspury & Yardley Gobion, Northamptonshire 1690-1920* was prompted by his desire to chronicle the early days of this Independent church so that its important place in the life of the village was appreciated and not forgotten. It was published in 2017.

An illustrated history of

The Protestant Dissenting Church Potterspury & Yardley Gobion Northamptonshire 1690-1920

Jack Clamp

TSL Publications

Second edition published in Great Britain in 2017
By TSL Publications, Rickmansworth

ISBN / 978-1-911070-79-5

Contents

Acknowledgments

About Jack Clamp

Page

List of Illustrations   6

An Introduction   7

The Origins of the Church: 1690-1778   15

Potterspury in the Evangelical Revival:
1778-1825   32

James Slye and the Victorian Chapel:
1825-1873   39

The Late Victorian, Edwardian & Georgian
Chapel: 1875-1920   45

APPENDICES

Table 1: Children in Independent Sunday
School, Potterspury   41

Appendix A: The Church Covenants   52

Appendix B: Some Notable Dates   60

Appendix C: Succession of Ministers   65

Appendix D: Trustees of Potterspury
and Yardley Gobion Congregational
Church 1714-1902   67

Appendix E: Names Given at Baptism
1740-1857 (100 years)   70

Bibliography   73

List of Illustrations

Potterspury Chapel and Manse	Cover
Dr Edmund Calamy	Page 8, 17
Caroline Wood	Page 12
Pastor and Deacons	Page 13
Village Couple	Page 13
Meeting of NBC Union Assembled at Potterspury	Page 14
Old Meeting/Pastor's House	Page 19
Dr Philip Doddridge	Page 25
Chapel and Manse	Page 33
Revd Ebenezer White	Page 35
Revd James Slye	Page 40
Yardley Gobion Chapel with Modern Front	Page 43
Chapel Poster	Page 49
James White & Wife	Page 50
Orchestra in Front of Chapel	Page 51
James White by Chapel	Page 51
Revd Angel and Deacons	Page 52

An Introduction

After Henry VIII broke away from the Roman Catholic Church in 1529, as Head of the new Church of England he introduced certain changes in its organisation and doctrine, but he remained basically conservative in his religious thinking. However, there were from the outset those who wanted much more thorough-going changes, and these radicals got their way for a time during the reign of Henry's son, the boy king Edward VI: for example, the Prayer Book was translated into English, to be used in all churches, clergy were allowed to marry, and altars were moved to the centre of the church, not separated from the congregation at the east end. Edward's sister Elizabeth was more circumspect and tried to steer a middle way between the "High Church" Anglicans who wanted the church to remain much as it had been for hundreds of years before 1529, and the "Puritans" who wanted more fundamental organisational and doctrinal changes.

Under the first two Stuarts, conflict between these two groups intensified and by 1642 religion was one of the issues that divided Royalists and Parliamentarians in the Civil War. By this time there were two sorts of radical: those who remained members of the church and agitated for reform from within, and those who refused to attend church at all, and tried to set up their own organisations outside it.

After the Civil War the established church was dismantled and there was a period of experiment, but by 1660 people were by and large tired of experiment and were prepared to have the Church of England restored along with the Crown, provided that minority could worship as they pleased. Charles II accepted this. However, the first Parliament of his reign was conservative and although it acknowledged the existence of Nonconformists (those who refused to worship in the traditional way and wanted their own, independent, chapels), Parliament passed laws, known as the "Clarendon Code", which made life very difficult for them.[1]

The clergy were to conform by St. Bartholomew's Day, 24 August 1662, a date purposely chosen so that if they failed to do so they would lose a half-year's tithes and even worse, be ejected from their house and living. About 2,000 clergymen did not conform and as a consequence were ejected. This action caused great hardship especially to those who had a wife and children to support and in some cases clergy conformed, when they might have done otherwise, had it not been for these dire consequences. Among those who were ejected but later conformed to keep his living, which was not worth more than £30 a year was, according to Dr Calamy,[2] the Vicar of the Established Church at Potterspury, Joseph Nevill.[3]

Dr Edmund Calamy

Things improved somewhat for Nonconformists in 1689, when William III replaced James II. The Nonconformists were given permission to worship in their own chapels, but they were still banned from holding any office under the Crown (the Test and Corporation Acts), and they were not allowed to open their own schools or academies. However, this was a great break-through compared with the rest of Europe, and there were further advances in toleration, both at national and local levels, during

[1] GV Mawer MA (2010) *A short history of Nonconformity*
[2] Dr Edmund Calamy MA DD, The English Presbyterian churchman and historian who wrote an important account of the Church of England ministers who were ejected for not conforming in 1662
[3] Calamy's Continuation, vol 2, p 664

the eighteenth century. By this time the main Nonconformist groups were Baptists, Independents (later known as Congregationalists) and Quakers, to which were added during the course of the century, Methodists. In 1828 the Test and Corporation Acts were repealed, ending the exclusion of Nonconformists from politics and society.

It is inevitable that the story of the rise of religious dissent, and in particular the founding of the Dissenting Church at Potterspury, should be very much concerned with the leading figures of the time, who together with many others suffered extreme hardship, especially in the early days, following their decision not to conform. At the same time, one must not overlook the important part played by the ordinary members, many of whom were poor farm labourers together with their families, who in many cases risked persecution, fines or even imprisonment for failing to observe the conditions of the Act of Uniformity which made attendance at the restored Church of England compulsory (with a fine for being absent without reasonable excuse) and the Conventicle Act of 1664 forbidding all religious meetings other than those of the Anglican Church.

In spite of this Act, people still continued to meet illegally which, five years later, prompted the Archbishop of Canterbury, Archbishop Sheldon, to instigate an enquiry into the extent of these conventicles. A report to the Bishop of Peterborough by John Palmer, the Archdeacon of Northampton, giving an account of the *Conventicles held in the 7 Western Deanryes of the Diocese of Peterborough* includes four villages in South Northamptonshire, viz. Passenham, Old Stratford, Yardley Gobion and Blisworth, linked together.[4] It lists 50 or 60 semi-Anabaptists frequently meeting at Passenham (but mostly from other parishes) on Sundays at Mr Harrison's, and goes on to say that "the same also meet at Old Stratford at Robert Scot's. Their headquarters is said to be at Yardley Gobion where they meet every Sunday where a Mr Hartly of Stony Stratford, a draper

4 N[orthampton] R[ecord] O[ffice]: Conventicles held in the Western Deanryes of the Diocese of Peterborough, 1669

(a Captain in the last warres[sic]) is commonly said to be their leader". Here the connection is clearly made between dissent and subversion. Yardley Gobion was at that time a hamlet in the parish of Potterspury, as was Old Stratford, but no mention is made of Potterspury as a meeting place. This may be accounted for by the fact that, as reported by the Archdeacon, "it is a rare thing to find a conventicle or any numbers of Separatists in any Town where there lives a Justice of the Peace, or Lord of the Manor whose interest in the town is considerable". Many of the people may well have also attended the Established Church and kept their other activities secret. It would appear that these so-called Anabaptists were at some time connected with the Baptist Church at Stony Stratford, Bucks (just half a mile from Old Stratford) which had its origin as early as 1625 and whose members had suffered much and been sent to gaol for their nonconformity and often had to meet in nearby fields or woods in spite of having built a small chapel capable of holding about 100 people.[5]

The Archdeacon in his summary to the report says:

> … for their authority (for thinking they did not offend) the Quakers and Anabaptists pretend the spirit and the light of God is within them; the Independents and Presbyterians their calling is from God and that they ought to obey God rather than men; and woe is to me if I preach not the Gospel.

This may go some way to explain why some people were prepared to break these laws even though in doing so it could and did result in persecution. The changes they saw taking place in the Established Church led many to the opinion that the Church was diverging from the Protestant cause and they were offended by what they saw as the advance of Popery. The Church was developing a theology of its own divergent from that of other Protestants and began to insist that the Church was itself a source of spiritual truth no less than the Bible. This was unacceptable to many people, who thus became dissenters.

5 Nonconformists Memorial, vol 3, p 47

In his attempt to downgrade those who attended the conventicles the Archdeacon writes dismissively:

> For their condition there is scarce any gentlemen of £100 per annum that forsakes the church, nor 10 yeomen of that estate that I can find. Few men of £50 a year. There are far more women than men. Many children and servants. And there be many prophane [sic] persons who often flock to the doors and windows out of curiosity and make their numbers seem greater than they are.

As far as it is possible to discover from the scant records, the number of members admitted into the Independent Church at Potterspury from the end of the 17th century up to the end of the 19th century was 427. Of these, 293 were females as opposed to 134 males so one can appreciate the large support given by these women but, except for one or two references, very little mention is made of their contribution to the cause or any part they took in any serious discussion in the early days. Sometimes some were formed into a committee to arrange the tea for some special occasion such as the celebration, in 1880, of the centenary of the building of the chapel and manse. They of course played a large part in the running of the Sunday School. As the 19th century drew to a close women had begun to be more self-assertive throughout the country leading eventually to them being given the vote and this mood is reflected in their voice being heard more often and the greater part being played by the women in the affairs of the church. In 1892, on 21 September, the Church Minutes record for the first time that the pastor's wife, Mrs White, proposed a motion with regard to admission of a new member, which was seconded by Miss Wood. From that time on, women members of the congregation quite often proposed and seconded motions at church meetings.

Some of the more affluent lady members sometimes left considerable sums of money to the Church. In 1886 Mrs Ann Scrivener of Deanshanger left a £40 legacy to the church to be invested by them and the yearly income to be paid to the minister. Mrs Sarah Iliffe, who had been an active member for many years (particularly concerning herself with the younger members of the church), bequeathed in her will of 1910 a sum of £50 to be used towards the purchase of a new organ for the Congregational Chapel. Another staunch supporter of the church for 51 years, until her death in November 1914, was Miss Caroline (Carrie) Mary Wood (who became a member during Slye's ministry, in 1863); a Sunday School teacher and Treasurer, and Secretary of the local branch of the London

Caroline Wood

Missionary Society. In her will she left the sum of £300 for the conversion of an old stone outbuilding (a photograph of which hangs in the vestry) into an institute which the church decided to call, in her memory, the Wood Memorial Institute. The new building was completed by February 1916 and remained in use, not only by the church but by many village societies; at one time it was used by the village school as a woodwork centre. Regretfully, it has now fallen into disrepair and is to be sold. Against her name in the Register of Members, the Revd W Angel wrote, after her death, "She rests from her labours & her works do follow her." She also left a sum of £400 to the church which was originally invested in Government War Loan stock at 4½%. Generally speaking however, the vast majority of members were far from wealthy. Many of the men worked as agricultural labourers on local farms or the Grafton estate and the women and children were lacemakers or servants. The opening of the Railway Works at Wolverton in the early 19th century gave employment to many men and therefore the population's incomes improved.

During periods of crisis, particularly when the church was without a pastor, the Deacons and Trustees devoted themselves to the task of maintaining the continuity of the cause at Potterspury, sometimes for several years. In the late 19th century the names of Sam Valentine (miller), Alfred Scrivener (miller), Job Scrivener (miller), Joseph Holloway (tailor), Albert Gray (clerk of works to the Duke of Grafton), and Joseph Wood (farmer) are those often mentioned in this respect. The other responsibility of the Deacons was to see that the members abided by the rules of the church and that they attended regularly. Any transgressions such as drunkenness or swearing were swiftly dealt with and the offending person suspended from communion until he or she repented and showed, to the Deacons' satisfaction, true contrition. If the offence was com-

Pastor and Deacons

mitted again then they would most likely be cut off from the church and expelled. More serious misdemeanours such as thieving, fornication, adultery, improper conduct, or imprudence would bring instant suspension, sometimes to be followed by dis-

missal. One such offence was committed by a girl member who was considered to be imprudent in having a young man to see her on the Sabbath evening and sitting up with him all night. In all probability, she was suspended not only on moral grounds but equally because he was not a member of the church. Marriage with non-members was frowned upon at that time. Interestingly, the *Register of Baptisms*, 1739-1918, does not contain one entry of an illegitimate child.

Village Couple

The beliefs and practices of the true Nonconformists were very much a part of their everyday life and influenced their behaviour and the way they conducted themselves to a great extent. This sometimes brought them into conflict with others who did not share their belief that God was to be obeyed rather than man, and also the preaching of the gospel was of paramount importance. Intolerance and hostility by others was spoken of by the Revd JH Baker from Marsh Gibbon when addressing the 1906 Spring meeting of the North Bucks Congregational Union assembled at Potterspury. *The Northampton Mercury* reports that he spoke of "... the peculiar difficulties under which nonconformity existed in country places, arising from the rule of the parson and Conservative squire. There were many farms, he said, over whose gates, when they were empty, the legend might as well be written: No Nonconformist Need Apply. And the country tradesmen, as well as farmers who were Nonconformists, knew well what intimidation was."

Meeting of the North Bucks Congregational Union assembled at Potterspury

The Origins of the Church: 1690-1778

Following the Toleration Act of 1689, which confirmed what King James had granted by prerogative in 1687 and which allowed nonconformist meetings to be held providing the meeting place had been registered, from 1690 an attempt was made to establish an Independent Congregation at Potterspury by Michael Harrison from Caversfield near Bicester in Oxfordshire.[6] Caversfield was at that time in Buckinghamshire. It was transferred to Oxfordshire in 1844. The Presbyterian churchman and historian, Dr Edmund Calamy, DD (1671-1732) was in 1691 studying at Oxford. He tells of walking from Bicester, where he had been preaching, to Caversfield where he preached in the public church there. He says, "Harrison usually preached in the church there, of which his relative, Maximilian Bard was patron, and that he lived in the house adjoining. But Mr Harrison was now at a great distance from home [and] in Northamptonshire where he was gathering a congregation of nonconformists about Potterspury, designing to quit the Church and settle among them".[7] According to Calamy, the people about Potterspury were building him a meeting house, with a dwelling house adjoining. Baker throws some doubt as to whether Harrison was strictly a clergyman of the established church, or simply officiated without Episcopal institution under the sanction of his relative, the patron, who was a Presbyterian.[8] Browne Willis describes Mr Harrison as "a

6 NRO: The Meeting Minute Book of the Congregation of Protestant Dissenters Assembling in Potterspury in the County of Northampton 1740-1892

7 E Calamy (RT Rutt, ed) (1829) *A Historical Account of My Own Life*, pp 300-1

8 NRO: G Baker, *History & Antiquities of the County of Northampton*, vol 2

Dissenting teacher who belonged to the Presbyterian family of the Bards".[9] Walter Wilson also refers to Harrison as a Presbyterian[10] but Slye in his church history questions this, as Potterspury and later St. Ives, Cambridgeshire, where he went after leaving Potterspury, were *in his opinion*, Independent Churches.[11] However, it will be seen from earlier references that some considered him to be a Presbyterian, and in 1715 reference is made to St. Ives Presbyterian Meeting House where he is said to have had a congregation of 500 persons. He also received an annual sum from the Presbyterian Fund Board.[12] In 1679 he is listed as Curate in charge at Caversfield, James Durant being the Vicar at that time. The Caversfield church register contains this entry,[13]

> Michael Harrison, minister of the gospel, and Miss Ann Bateman, daughter of John Bateman, gentleman, of Spilsbury, in the parish of Harrington and County of Derby, wear [sic] married the twenty-first day of July, 1681, by Mr Allcock, Curate of Googtry [Goostrey?], in the county of Chester att [sic] Longner [Longnor?] in the county of Staford' Five children of this marriage were baptised at Caversfield between 1682 and 1689. Rebecah in 1682, Eulaliah in 1683, Bateman in 1685, Martha in 1688, and Joseph in 1689.

After the entry of three names, the scribe has added to the register: "These 3 wear [sic] the children of Michael Harrison, minister of Caversfield".

It is not at all clear as to why Harrison went to Potterspury. There is no doubt that there were many dissenters in the area about Potterspury and their headquarters was said to be at Yardley Gobion. There is no reason to believe that the numbers had decreased by the time of Harrison's arrival. With a wife

9 JC Blomfield (1893) *History of Deanery at Bicester* pp 40-1

10 Walter Wilson, *History & Antiquities of Dissenting Churches*, vol 3 pp 393, 480

11 NL: Revd James Slye (1831) *A Brief History of the Rise and Progress of the Independent Church at Potterspury*

12 Mary Wagner (1982) *Not an Easy Church*

13 *Caversfield Parish Church Register*

and five children to support and the fact that his patron died in 1690, he may have felt the need for a more settled home and the need for financial support. The *Common Fund Survey 1690-92*,[14] referring to Mr Harrison, notes that: "att Pottersperry, the people there have undertaken to provide him a maintenance." This would seem to indicate that the church had attracted some members at least who were wealthy enough to provide sufficient funds and therefore no payment was required from the Common Fund. However, the survey does state that "Pottersperry, where Mr. Harrison is fixing, desire some assistance towards repairing their meeting house."

Dr Edmund Calamy

He and his family probably removed to Potterspury in 1691 or 1692 although a bibliography published in 1916[15] suggests that he was still at Caversfield in 1694 which disagrees with both Dr Calamy and the *Common Fund Survey* which talk of him being at Potterspury in 1691.

When the barn, which formed the Meeting House at Potterspury, was fitted out, Dr Calamy says, "I at their request preached the Lord's Day and had a numerous auditory. I was sometimes, there afterwards."[16]

This is how the early history is described in an account written in the first *Church Minute Book*.[17]

It is supposed Mr. Harrison the first pastor was an ejected minister. He came hence from Cavesfield near Bicester Oxf. Mr. Warr (great grandfather of Thos Warr now a member) came from that part to enjoy the benefit of Mr. Harrison's Ministry. Mr. H brought a Pulpit from the place of worship where he labord [sic]

14 NRO: Common Fund Survey, 1690-95
15 WT Whitley (1916) *A Baptist Biography* p 219
16 *Op.cit.* n 3
17 *Op.cit.* n 2

before & Mr. Warr being a shoemaker contrived to have it filled with shoe peggs [sic], one of wch [sic] was equal in size to 3 or 4 of the modern ones. It was brought with his goods in a waggon [sic] from Bicester.

Harrison was not strictly speaking an ejected minister. The Thomas Warr mentioned in the above account became a member in 1786 so it could not have been written before that date, almost one hundred years after the event. In 1801, when a new set of church regulations was introduced, one of the signatories to it was Thomas Warr of Pury. Members by the name of Warr were active in the church for many years as evidenced by the name appearing in various registers. In 1881, Thomas Warr, a coal merchant of Yardley Gobion, was appointed a Trustee of the chapel at Potterspury and in 1895 a Trustee of the chapel at Yardley Gobion. Sarah Warr, who was made a member in 1888, appears to be the last one of that name to be so. Her name is included in a Roll of Church Members dated 1913.

Harrison collected a congregation from the nearby villages, probably containing members from the conventicles reportedly held locally from at least 1669. The North Bucks Association[18] in 1820 gives the date as 1658. Some of these people had been connected with the Anabaptists at Stony Stratford but Mr Harrison's sentiments did not lie with them so this may have excluded a few. However, allegiances were still very fluid and the hearers were more concerned with good preaching than doctrine.

In 1694 he was the author of a work published in London which leaves no doubt as to his thoughts on the matter, entitled *Infant Baptism, God's Ordinance; or Clear Proofs that all the Children of Believing Parents are in the Covenant of Grace, and have as much Right to Baptism, as the Children of the Jews had to Circumcision, the then Seal of the Covenant.* Whatever provoked Mr Harrison to attack the beliefs of his new neighbours is not

---

[18] Dr Williams' Library, London: *The Proceedings and Reports of the North Bucks Association of Independent Churches and Ministers 1818-1829*

known but that they were not entirely unmoved is evident from the title page of the work being transcribed into their own Church Book and after the words *Preacher of the Gospel at Potterspury, as Mr. Harrison has stiled himself* they wrote "as he says". His attack did not go unanswered and although the good people of Stony Stratford had no minister, in a short time it was answered by a Mr Collins to whom Mr Harrison replied in a letter in which it was said he wrote many uncharitable reflections and scandalous aspersions on the Baptists in general. In 1697, an answer to the publication was written and published in London under the title *A Vindication of the Baptized Churches, from the Calumnies of Mr. Michael Harrison. By William Russell, M.D. A Lover of Primitive Christianity.* It would appear, however, that the matter was carried no further.[19]

Old Meeting / Pastor's House

Although in the past the nonconformists had had to support each other in times of prejudice and persecution, it would seem that following the 1689 Toleration Act when dissenters were acknowledged as citizens, albeit second class ones, the various factions were far from united. The church records show that for much of its early life there were very few members from Potterspury itself; most members coming from Towcester, Hanslope, Paulerspury, Stony Stratford and of course Yardley Gobion, which was at that time part of Potterspury. The meetings were held in the barn or outhouse, adjoining a residence belonging to Richard Scrivener, yeoman, which had, as has already been mentioned, been fitted up as a place of worship at the people's own expense.

In 1691 Mr Harrison bought most of this estate, known as Pedder's Farm, from Richard Scrivener, for £70 and Harrison

---

[19] *Op.cit.* n 6 p 393

and his wife settled in Potterspury.[20] It has been suggested that he used money realised by the sale of a small estate in the county of Chester, which was his wife's marriage portion. However, it was not until June 1694 that a deed was drawn up relating to a marriage settlement between Harrison and his wife Ann on one part and Richard Bateman and John Milward of Derbyshire which deals with the sale of property in Cheshire and mention is made of the purchase of Pedder's Farm. The witnesses were John, Joan, and Moses Warr.[21]

The Revd Harrison, in addition to his other attributes, was an author and hymn-writer. In 1691 he published *Several Sermons on Justification* and *The Believer's Marriage with Christ*.[22] By 1700 he had published *Twelve Divine Hymns: Composed for the Lord's Table, and the Lord's Day*. In an address in the *Christian Reader*, Harrison says, "Tis a great Pity that so many otherwise Well-meaning Christians, should yet have a Prejudice against singing Psalms, Hymns, and Spiritual Songs, with Conjoyned Voices in Publick Assemblies; Whereas it has always been the Practice of the Church of God, both under the Old and New Testament. Christ Sung at his Last Supper." This prejudice is an example of the non-acceptance by some people at that time of anything other than the scriptures. There was a deep suspicion in the culture of dissent of anything smacking of the theatre, or of "art", unless the devotional element was very plain. Referring to his own hymns and being conscious that some at Potterspury might object to them, Harrison wrote: "If any dislike them, they are free to let them alone; And if ever I use any of them at the Lord's Table, it shall be with the Universal Consent of every one: The Lord tune our Hearts as well as Voices, to this sweet duty." John Taylor describes his hymns as having "true musical rhythm and clearly showing the note of praise".

The following is an example of this:

[20] The United Reformed Church Archives, London: Potterspury & Yardley Gobion United Reformed Church, Northants
[21] *Ibid.*
[22] The Bodleian Library, Oxford: Catalogue entry for Michael Harrison, minister of Potters-Pury

Most Glorious God and King,
Our Hearts to thee we'll Raise,
And Joyfully we'll Sing,
To thee sweet Songs of Praise;
For thou hast given
Thy own dear son, Man to become
Sent down from Heaven.

At the parliamentary election of 1702, Harrison voted for Earl Spencer and Sir St. Andrew St. John. At the 1705 election he voted for Lord Mordant and Sir St. Andrew St. John.[23] All three candidates were Whigs who advocated toleration of all Protestant Churches, but unfortunately for the dissenters they were not elected.

Harrison is said to have left Potterspury in 1709 to become the minister of an Independent Church at St. Ives, in Cambridgeshire, remaining there until his death in January 1726/7. However, according to the Burials Register of St. Ives' parish church, there is the probability that he removed to St. Ives around 1706 because his wife was buried there in 1706. He later remarried. A deed dated November 1709, which may have given the false impression that this was the date he moved, confirms that he was then at St. Ives. In June 1710, Mr Harrison sold the premises at Potterspury (including the house, which at that time was occupied by Isaac Robinson) to one John Gough of Highgate, Middlesex for £83,[24] "excepting and reserving out of this present grant the pulpit and all the seats, pews and galleries now standing and being within the said meeting house unto the only use of the congregation of people that belong to the said meeting house". It would appear that Mr Scrivener was still occupying and farming some of the property.

In 1714 the members obtained a 21 year lease on the property from John Gough at a rent of £4.10s per annum. The signatories to this agreement were John Saywell of Luffield Abbey, yeoman; John Watts, John Wickens and Edward Gray of

[23] NRO: 1/78 *Poll Books of Northampton for Knights of the Shire*, 1702, 1705
[24] *Op.cit.* n 17

Paulerspury, yeomen; Thomas Foukes of Towcester, collar maker; Henry Rockingham and William Addington of Potterspury, chandlers; and Hugh Boswell of Yardley Gobion.

In 1732 Gough and his wife Ann apparently sold the premises for £105 to John Saywell of Luffield Abbey, yeoman; Richard Scrivener of Potterspury, yeoman; John Wicken, John Buncher of Paulerspury, yeomen; Richard Brown and John Smith of Yardley Gobion, yeomen; Henry Brown of Stony Stratford, cordwainer; William Addington and Edward Scrivener of Potterspury, flax dressers; William Warr of Potterspury, cordwainer; William Hawley, John Hawley and Robert Howlett the younger of Paulerspury, carpenters; John Bitcheno of Paulerspury, sneathmaker; John Bland of Yardley Gobion, carpenter; and John Warr of Yardley Gobion, shoemaker.[25] The premises were to be held in trust by these people "who would suffer such preacher and teacher of the separate congregation of Protestant Dissenters as shall be allowed and approved by two third parts in number of the said (names as above) to inhabit and dwell in the said capital messuage or tenement and also do and shall from time to time permit and suffer such preacher and teacher of the separate congregation of Protestant Dissenters as shall be allowed and approved of as aforesaid to teach and preach in the said meeting house adjoining ... to do and perform all other Arts of Religious worship therein". Provision was also made for the replacement of trustees who may have died, by two thirds of those remaining, so that the number remained at sixteen. Over the years the church was very lax in carrying out these provisions and often the trustees fell to as little as two in number as they had by 1776 when these remaining two, John Bitcheno and John Smith, in consideration of their old age and certainty of death, nominated 25 trustees including themselves.

Mr Harrison was succeeded by the Revd Mr Bennett, of whom little is known, who declined to take the pastoral office and soon departed, to be followed by the Revd Isaac Robinson

---

[25] *Ibid.*

22

who, Slye says, remained for about four years.[26] Only one new member was admitted during this time. Some indication of the state of the church during this period, or at least one person's opinion of it, is given in an account in the records of College Street Church, Northampton by one Elizabeth Shepherd who, in December 1710, was proposing communion with them. She was required to give her reasons, before she could be accepted at Northampton, why she should leave the people at Potterspury. Her first reason was the fact that she lived some way from Potterspury but her main reason she gave as her dissatisfaction with their communion and discipline, they being, in her words, "… wide Presbyterians, the Pastor (when they had one) taking in persons, without any account of their faith being given by them to ye people, and when they have no Pastor (as at this present) they do not keep up any Order or anything of a Church State but account themselves at liberty to go where they please, ye Brethren never so much as praying together publickly." Her report that they had no pastor at this time conflicts with Slye's account. The College Street Church considered the meeting at Potterspury "… not to be a church rightly formed, nor in gospel-order, nor maintaining any power in themselves to admit or dismiss members etc." and judged, therefore, that her way was clear to leave them and theirs to receive her.[27]

By 1714 the Revd William Bushnell (born at Wallingford, Berks on March 3rd 1690) who had just completed his studies under the Revd John Moore of Bridgwater, Somerset, was the Pastor and, according to the *Evans List* of 1715-1717,[28] he was said to be a Presbyterian and receiving £6 from the Common Fund. Baker[29] says that he raised a large society at Potterspury, chiefly of the lower-classes, which is partly borne out by the *Evans List* which says that there were 500 hearers there but as

[26] *Op.cit.* n 7
[27] NRO: Records of College Street Church, Northampton
[28] NRO: Evans, *List of Dissenting Congregations* c1715-17
[29] *Op.cit.* n 4

this number included 20 parliamentary voters the standing of at least some members could hardly be considered lower-class. Of course they would not all be living at Potterspury. The *Church Minute Book*[30] lists 24 members admitted during his pastorate. He refused to quit his congregation for a more wealthy one at Bristol, and continued to preach at Potterspury until he exhausted his private patrimony in relieving their wants, when he removed to Andover, Hampshire in 1729 and then to Nailsworth, Gloucestershire in 1732. His relation, Dr Boulton, Archbishop of Armagh, greatly esteemed him for his piety, and offered him preferment in the Anglican Church, if he would conform, but Bushnell did not accept the offer and died in May 1744 having been appointed, a few months before, the pastor of the chapel of Maid Lane, Southwark. Six years passed before the next pastor, Samuel Tailor (probably a student from Samuel Benion's Academy, Shrewsbury) was ordained in 1735. It was said of him that he was a gentleman of considerable abilities but supposed to be somewhat disordered in his head. The *Church Minute Book*[31] lists 19 new members received during his time. He removed to Long Melford, Suffolk sometime before 1739.

John Heywood from Lincolnshire was invited to become the pastor in 1739 and after working in the village for twelve months was ordained on 25 September 1740. It was the custom in those days for the candidate for ordination to defend a thesis and Mr Heywood's subject was *The Scripture's a Rule of Faith*, which he maintained, as a proof of his learning, in Latin. At that time there were 57 members including fifteen who had been members in Mr Harrison's time, and one wonders what they made of it! The Revd Mr Petto, of Flore, Mr Cartwright, of Long Buckby, and the Revd Mr Drake, of Yardley. Hastings, led the devotions; the Revd Mr Clarke, of St. Albans, ordered the ordination prayer; the Revd Dr Doddridge, of Northampton, gave the charge. (Doddridge, in a letter to his wife, Mercy,

---

30 *Op.cit.* n 4
31 *Op.cit.* n 2

mentions going to Potterspury for the ordination of John Heywood.)[32] Finally, the Revd Mr Hunt, of Hackney, preached to the people. Mr Heywood's settlement at Potterspury was the commencement of a new era in the history of the Independents in Potterspury, which lasted for almost the next forty years of the 18th century.

A meeting of members of an Association of Northamptonshire ministers was held at Potterspury in 1741 at which Doddridge preached on "The Danger of Neglecting the Souls of Men". He returned to Potterspury to baptise Heywood's son, John Leaver, on 23 August 1744.

Mr Heywood, like Mr Harrison, also composed hymns for his congregation. He wrote forty-two in all and these were published in London in 1740 under the title *Hymns or Spiritual Songs, Chiefly taken from the Holy Scriptures* and were dedicated to his friend, the renowned Dr Philip Doddridge (a more famous hymn writer). It is worth noting that Heywood, as evidenced by its inclusion in the title, was still conscious of possible objection to anything not strictly from the Holy Scriptures. He wrote a hymn for his ordination service which began:-

> Proclaim the Love, adore the Grace,
> That guilty Sons of Adam's Race,
> Shall thus be honour'd of their God,
> To spread their Saviour's Name abroad.

Dr Philip Doddridge

There is no way of knowing what tune was used but it nicely fits *Winchester New* which was adapted from a chorale in a Lutheran tune book of 1690!

By all accounts, throughout his life he used his talents and his undoubted energy in striving to spread his Saviour's name abroad. He undoubtedly had the zeal and energy to preside over and minister to a congregation formed of individuals residing in no less than nineteen towns and

[32] NRO: Geoffrey F Nuttall (1978) *The correspondence of Philip Doddridge 1702-1751*

hamlets and evidently spent much of his time, when not in Potterspury, travelling round the district giving lectures and visiting and praying with his hearers. Josiah Bull in his book *Memorials of the Rev. William Bull*[33] says that John Heywood was the nephew of the celebrated nonconformist preacher Oliver Heywood who, according to J Hunter's *Life of Oliver Heywood* (1842), in thirty-five years travelled on average 900 miles a year preaching round neighbouring towns and villages; so it seems entirely appropriate for his nephew to continue in a like manner. John Heywood also practised fasting on certain important days – as his uncle did.

John Taylor writing in 1891 says of Heywood that "He was a man of great eccentricity, but of no little shrewdness, and was I imagine, even a genius in Ministry. His lank figure on horseback, with the loose ends of his unfastened neck-cloth flying about him, was a familiar sight in many villages around". The Revd Slye[34] was indeed fortunate enough to have access to and able to quote from Heywood's journal, which now, regretfully, appears to be lost, in which he recorded all the places at which he preached, as well as the houses he visited or stayed at for a night. Slye quotes as follows:

> Lord's Day, April 7th, 1771, a most merciful Sabbath, very hoarse, carried through: blessed be my dear Redeemer. — Luffield Abbey Lecture — Dear Jesus, smile and crown.
> Monday, April 8th, prayed at Luffield, and went to Mr. Hipwell's.
> Tuesday, April 9th. Burton Lecture — Dear Jesus, crown.
> Wednesday, April 10th. Cranford Lecture: Mr. John Ludborow buried — Lord, fit me to follow.
> Thursday, April 11th, prayed at Mrs. Ludborow's, and at Mrs. Pulver's: came to Thrupp, preached the evening lecture — Dear Jesus, smile and crown.
> Friday, April 12th, prayed at Mr. Hipwell's, came safe home, found all well — Bless the Lord, O my soul,

[33] NL: Josiah Bull (1864) *Memorials of the Revd William Bull*
[34] *Op.cit.* n 2

through my dear Redeemer. Amen.
Saturday, April 13th, at home, prayed at EGDG.
Lord's Day, April 14th, Towcester day: Stoney Stratford
Lecture: prayed and lodged at Mrs. Brown's: very hoarse
— Dear Jesus, appear.

However, the *Birth and Baptism Register*[35] of his time gives
further indication of the extent of his travels and influence
when one finds baptisms of children from many different villages and towns not only in Northamptonshire, Buckinghamshire, Bedfordshire and Hertfordshire but as far afield as
Lincolnshire and Rutland. An indication of Heywood's power
as a preacher is given by the case of two men, William
Boughton from Thornton, Bucks. and Thomas Strange (Slye
gives his name as John but Thomas is the name given in the
Minute Book) of Shalston, Bucks. who would walk nearly ten
miles to hear him preach at Potterspury where, in 1744, they
became members of the Independent Church. No doubt with
Heywood's influence and help they became pupils of Philip
Doddridge at the Dissenting Academy, Northampton. According to Slye this was in 1745 but a more accurate date would be
1747 as given in *A List of Pupils educated by P. Doddridge, D.D.*
supplied by Thomas Stedman in 1815 from a list made by Job
Orton (a pupil, friend, and biographer of Doddridge) which
also confirms the name Thomas Strange. Boughton eventually
became a pastor at Buckingham and Strange a pastor at Kilsby,
Northants, where he remained for 33 years. Strange was to
return to Potterspury in 1782 to take part in the ordination
service of John Goode who succeeded Heywood as pastor.

Heywood's loyalty to his Sovereign, his love of literature, and
his simplicity of heart attracted the notice of the neighbouring
nobility. Earl Temple[36] was considered to be a good friend who
often invited him to his home at Stowe, and the Duke of

[35] NRO: *The Register Book Concerning the Baptizing of Infants belonging to the Congregation of
Protestant Dissenters Assembling in Potters Pury in the Country of Northamptonshire 1739-
1918*
[36] Earl Temple, Viscount Cobham (1669?-1749). Rebuilt house at Stowe and laid
out the famous gardens.

Grafton[37] gave him free access to his library at Wakefield Lodge. In those days such a privilege would have been a great asset to any scholar. From 1738 he was a subscriber to *The Northamptonshire Book Society*, a society lending to its members books considered of merit. Doddridge was a fellow subscriber, and two books (Daniel Waterland's *Sermons* published in 1742 and Samuel Squire's *Enquiry into the Foundation of the English Constitution* published in 1745, now in the library of New College, London) contain both Doddridge's and Heywood's names. He was also a subscriber to *The Family Expositor* which Doddridge published from 1738 until 1756. Doddridge wrote to Heywood in February 1746/7 "… hoping to see the Potterspury minister on the last Thursday of the month, to preach a preparation sermon".[38] Doddridge continued his correspondence with Heywood until at least 1751.

The story is told that on the accession of George III, in 1760, he and other Nonconformist ministers came to London to present an address of loyalty to the King at St. James's Palace. When he joined the others in the ante-room to the audience chamber they looked somewhat askance at his untidy appearance and were equally surprised to see Lord Temple engage in really friendly conversation with him. However, His Lordship detained him too long (perhaps it would be churlish to suggest that this was an intentional act) and the King was about to retire when Heywood, not to be thwarted, called out, "Stop, please your Majesty, stop! I have come all the way from Potterspury to kiss your Majesty's hand, and I hope I shall be allowed this honour". The King stopped and turned to Mr Heywood when it is said he kissed the King's hand two or three times and said emphatically, "God bless your Majesty; I hope you will make a good King".[39] Earlier that year, Heywood published in London *A Sermon on the Death of His late Majesty*

[37] Augustus Henry Fitzroy, 3rd Duke of Grafton (1735-1811), Prime Minister 1768-1770
[38] *Op.cit.* n 29
[39] *Op.cit.* n 7

King George II., preached at Potters Pury, October 26th 1760.

Unfortunately, he was less successful in choosing a marriage partner. Tradition says that both he and his wife acted dishonourably in that he married her knowing that she was already engaged to one of his friends and that she took advantage of her fiancé's absence to give her hand to the one under whose care she had been put. Slye[40] tells us that he was married about the time he came to Potterspury [1739] but further research suggests that he was married to Hannah Sewell on 16 October 1732 at St. Swithin's Church, Lincoln. The entry in the marriage register there says that he came from Stamford.[41] His wife, Hannah, proved to be a violent and selfish person and the effects of this unsuitable union were partly apparent in his neglected person and comfortless appearance. In his work as a minister of the gospel he was often impeded and rendered unhappy. His want of domestic comfort, may, however, have led him to seek in unwearied labours that comfort which he could not find at home.

Not until 1768, some twenty-eight years after their arrival at Potterspury, did he have the great happiness of seeing his wife admitted into church membership. On 1 April he recorded in the *Church Minute Book*, "My Dear Wife Mrs. Heywood desires to be admitted the next Sacrament Day but one". And on the following 21 May, he wrote, "My Dear Wife unanimously admitted".

He also obtained little comfort from his three children, two daughters and a son. One daughter, Martha, was baptised in 1741 and died in 1747. Her father wrote this footnote on the page recording her baptism, "This most dear and agreeable child died Sept. 20th 1747. It was the will of my Heavenly Father to translate her to Glory so soon, I hope and desire to submit".[42] His son, of whom he had hopes of his eventually joining the ministry, and who in 1762 he had placed under the

---

40 *Ibid.*

41 Lincolnshire Archives Office

42 *Op.cit.* n 32

care of Dr Ashworth in the Dissenting Academy at Daventry, drowned whilst bathing when only eighteen years of age. The remaining daughter was said to be no comfort or credit, being described as an ungodly child. It was not uncommon when he returned from his pastoral journeys, on entering the village, to be reproached with the sins or follies of those to whom he was related, viz. his wife and remaining daughter. Interestingly, there seems to be no other mention of this daughter and there is no entry for her in the baptism register at Potterspury which might indicate that she was born before coming to the village. If the writer's theory is correct and John Heywood was married in 1732, this is quite possible. There is an entry in the marriage register of the Potterspury Parish Church, dated 26 February 1762, recording the marriage, by licence, of one Mary Heywood to William Watts of All Saints parish, Northampton. The witnesses were JL Heywood and Richard Jones and the marriage was celebrated by the Revd Robert Harding, the vicar at that time.[43] JL Heywood is most likely her brother, John Leaver Heywood, not her father. It seems therefore that this remaining daughter's name was Mary and if so she may be the Mary Heywood who was baptised in the Gainsborough Presbyterian Nonconformist Church, Lincolnshire in August 1737 which would also explain why she is not recorded at Potterspury. Unfortunately the Gainsborough register does not give the parents' names but this is the same church at which Hannah Sewell (possibly Mary's mother) was baptised in 1710.[44] James Slye[45] says that after the death of John Heywood [1778], his daughter with her mother, left the village. But in July 1762 there is a baptism registered at Potterspury[46] of Mary, a daughter of William and Mary Watts of Long Buckby, and if they are the newly wed couple then it would seem that she had left the village some time before her father died, al-

[43] NRO: Register of Marriages, Potterspury Parish Church

[44] *Op.cit.* n 37

[45] *Op.cit.* n 7

[46] NRO: Register of Baptisms, Potterspury Parish Church

though of course she may have returned.

Slye writes that:

> At length Mr. Heywood's health began to decline, the effects of his frequent exposure to wet and cold, in his journies [sic] to preach in the villages, began to shew themselves upon his constitution; but still he could not be prevailed upon to give up his delightful work: his great fear was lest he should at last be accounted an idle servant, a loiterer in God's vineyard. As long therefore as he possibly could, he continued his journies; and when he could no longer take them, continued to preach at home; and when unable to ascend the pulpit, or even walk into the meeting, he would, like the Apostle John, be carried into the assembly, and being placed in his chair in one of the aisles, he would there exhort the people to come to Christ.[47]

Mr John Goode, at that period a student at Newport Academy, assisted Mr Heywood at this time. He eventually became pastor in 1782 after Heywood's death.

Heywood is said to have always displayed great affection and love of children and young persons. When confined to his bed, in his last sickness, he would have the young people in his charge assembled around his bedside where he addressed them and then laid his hands upon them. On 1 June 1778, while reportedly "surrounded by a few people he had selected to be with him, John Heywood fell asleep, in the Lord". His funeral sermon was preached at Potterspury by his friend the Revd William Bull of Newport Pagnell.[48]

A Church Covenant, to which newly enrolled members were expected to subscribe, was drawn up by Heywood and is written in his own hand in the Meeting Minute Book. A copy of this covenant is printed at the end of this account.

---

[47] *Op.cit.* n 7
[48] Congregational Magazine, November 1831

Potterspury in the
Evangelical Revival: 1778-1825

By the time of Heywood's death, the church membership had reduced to sixteen women and one man and all were aged. The church was without a Pastor until 1782 although John Goode, a student at Newport Pagnell Academy, deputised for a greater part of this time, as he had done some time before Mr Heywood's death. During this period, the old Meeting House (which had originally been a barn or outhouse) with the adjoining residence of the Minister, was pulled down and the present chapel, which Coleman[49] describes as having walls of brick in Flemish bond with blue headers at the front, rubble at the back and a tiled roof, was built in 1780. Pevsner[50] describes it as "a very pretty two storeyed brick range with dark chequered pattern." Apparently, the manse was built later in the same year. Although the two buildings abut each other and are of similar construction an inspection shows that there is no physical joint between the two buildings and in fact the brick courses do not even line up and each roof has a different pitch. With no pastor and a small, elderly membership one wonders how this mammoth task was financed and carried out, but the fine buildings they had erected still stand, with very few changes, as a memorial to their efforts.

John Goode was ordained Pastor in October 1782 and he was apparently very much respected by all who knew him and soon greatly increased the declining congregation. He remained in Potterspury until 1794 when he removed to the Independent

---

[49] Thomas Coleman (1853) *Memories of the Independent Churches in Northamptonshire*
[50] Nikolaus Pevsner, *The Buildings of England, Northamptonshire*

Church of Christ, at White Row, London which at that time had one of the best and largest nonconformist congregations in London, but this move proved to be an unfortunate one for John Goode, who was not successful there, and an equally unfortunate one for the church at Potterspury where, after his departure, a sad state of affairs soon existed. The members who resided at Towcester decided it more expedient to form themselves into a separate Church than to continue their attendance at Potterspury and were accordingly dismissed from the Church Meeting there.[51]

Mr Goode's successor, who had visited Potterspury before his departure, was George Vowell of the Academy at Homerton who was invited as a candidate for the pastoral charge. Judging from the contents of a letter he wrote to a friend, he seems to have preferred the rural life at Potterspury (which appears to have suited his taste and disposition) which he compares and judges to be preferable to the amusements and opportunities afforded by life in London when he writes, "I am quite happy in the expectation of an abode in Potterspury, where I can hear the rustling of trees, and not the rattling of chariot wheels: where I can listen to the nightingale's melodious notes, and not be offended with the drunkard's song: where I can enjoy a walk in the green fields, without the bustle and tumult of London streets: where I can enjoy the company of friends, without being

Chapel & Manse

exposed to the impertinent visits of triflers and gossips. You will smile, perhaps, at my monkish taste, and say, what is all this to a charming society, elegance, and amusements of various kinds, which a large and populous city affords: here is perpetual entertainment, always new, and ravishing delights, where all

[51] *Op.cit.* n 2

the senses may be gratified at a small expence [sic]."[52]

Unfortunately, it seems that some of those at Potterspury did not generally approve of him as a preacher and successor to Mr Goode but in spite of this it did not deter him from what he considered to be his duty to mankind. With this in view he paid particular attention to the instruction of the children of the poor and regularly set aside some time after Sunday services for that purpose. Soon after he arrived in Potterspury he was married to a Miss Hall and the newly-weds having a small amount of cash which they did not require determined to use it to help the poor. But, sad to relate, his health speedily declined and he soon returned to Brixton Causeway where he died some months afterwards at the age of twenty-three. The Revd Rowland Hill said that "had he lived he would have been a minister to be consulted".[53]

Mr Morrell, from the same Homerton Academy, preached at Potterspury until the end of the year when he removed to Kilsby. Early in 1795, the Revd William Whitefoot, of London, preached on several successive Sundays at Potterspury but because of a difference of opinion in the congregation with his doctrinal sentiments (unfortunately no mention is made of what these differences were), he departed for Hanslope, Bucks, taking with him the church members who lived there. In the period of about two years there was a succession of preachers, led by the Revd John Savage who soon departed, to be followed by the Revd John May who in turn was followed by Revd William Saunders all of whom were so unsuccessful that when Mr Ebenezer White was invited to take charge of the Independent Church in 1798 he was apparently faced with a difficult task as matters had fallen into a very low state. The church was in a very dilapidated condition (only 18 years after it was built) and the membership fallen from 47 to just eight.

In 1799 he reorganised the Church, made an abridgement of the Church Covenant, and continued to preach at Potterspury

---

[52] Letter shown to author in private collection
[53] *The Evangelical Magazine* 1795, pp 45-85

until 1800, although he never accepted the call to be pastor. Mr White composed a poem soon after he arrived in Potterspury in which he expressed his exasperation with his flock and his lack of success with them which somewhat contradicts Slye's comment about White having taken great pains with the people at Pury, by whom he was much respected. This poem gives us a fascinating glimpse of Ebenezer White's thinking about the state of things in the Independent Church at Potterspury at the end of the 18th century. It would appear that he lacked the common touch (surely so necessary for a pastor of an Independent church in a rural community at that time) and failed to understand his rustic and probably mostly illiterate flock, had scant regard for them and seems to have even held them in contempt. They in their turn seem to have had little respect for him or his teaching in spite of his obvious learning.

The poem runs as follows:

At Pury then, I join a rustic throng,
Blockish as inattentive. Not the house
Of God himself could awe them. In comes Hodge
As gently as a trooper; plump he squats
In his accustomed seat. The farmer snores;
His son looks big, and as dashing as a lord;
And ere the blessing closes with 'Amen',
An impious hubbub bounces on your ear;
And faster than they entered, all rush out.
But not with prayerful silence; no one asks,
With pensive earnestness, 'Am I the wretch
Thus guilty, or thus pardoned? Is heaven mine?'
But talk of weather, and the growth of corn,
Or scandal; the most trifling village news;
Such themes the intervals of worship fill.

Ye visit their abodes in the fond hope
Of finding life. You are discovered: one
In the stable lurks; one slinks behind a stack,

Revd Ebenez-
er White

Anxious to 'scape the parson, who perchance
Might start religion. Join their social throng;
Or at the dining board, or cheerful tea,
Bring up the subject of the last discourse –
The wisest cannot recollect the text!
But each devoutly tries: one fumbler thumbs
The bible; and what you in David read
Is certainly (they all conclude) in John.

Peasants have human souls; and he is blest
Who plucks but one from mis'ry and despair.
The rude and simple are to Jesus dear.
But when both young and long instructed shew
A vicious dominance, but female free!
When any name but that of Christ is sweet,
And any theme more grateful than his love;
Who'd plough a rock? or water a dead tree?
Or toil with souls gross-hearted, – sermon-proof? –
Perplexed, dispirited, as useless here,
In spite of house and orchard and some friends
Affectionate, and Fitzroy's transient smile,
I sigh for liberty, and fain would fly.

So oft we loathe the oaks ourselves desired,
And of our chosen gardens grew ashamed.

"Nevertheless at thy word I will let down the net". Isaiah 1.30.[54]

How frustrated he must have been when he wrote those last few lines. His mention of Fitzroy is interesting. Presumably he is referring to the Third Duke of Grafton who, according to the Revd. James Slye,[55] was in principle a Dissenter and subscribed £10 a year to the cause. The subscription was continued even after his death until the decease of the next pastor, Isaac Gardner.

After Mr White's departure, application was again made for assistance from Newport Pagnell and it is recorded that no person took a more lively interest in the concerns of the church

[54] NRS: Vide Paraliepomena; or the Remembrance of Former Days, a fragment in the Select Remains of the Rev E White, of Chester. See also *Northampton Past & Present*, 1980 vol vi no 3

[55] *Op.cit.* n 13

at that time than the Revd Mr Greathead,[56] then living at Newport Pagnell. Baker[57] says that he was a well known friend of the poet and hymn writer, William Cowper of Olney. A crucial meeting was held between four members of the church viz. Thomas Warr, George Wallis, Thomas Roote, and Joseph Church, and Mr Greathead at which they agreed it had become very necessary to decide on a united plan of action. They considered that the Church had been reduced to a very small number, and had been too long without a pastor, and had repeatedly appeared in danger of being deprived of the privileges of public worship, partly because of a want of acting unanimously as a Church of Christ and partly because of a lack of steadfast support by themselves and others who had formerly joined together. An eight-part resolution was drawn up (one suspects, in view of the quality of the language used, probably by the Revd Greathead) laying out the future conduct of the Church in all matters relating to the congregation and the public worship at the Independent Church at Potterspury.

Not until 1805 was the Revd Isaac Gardner, from Essex, recommended as a suitable pastor by Mr Greathead. This was a surprising recommendation when one considers that the *Church Meeting Minute Book* tells us that unfortunately Mr Gardner was not a young man and for the greater part of his 16 years at Pury he was said to be so infirm that he was unable to supply the zeal which was required to revitalise the cause. He did, however, find the necessary energy to help with the setting up of a separate Independent church at Stony Stratford which had the unfortunate effect of taking away those who were members of the church at Potterspury but lived at Stony Stratford, and so the congregation became smaller still. It is interesting to see that Gardner baptised 26 children from Stony Stratford out of a total of the 84 he baptised during his pastorate at Potterspury.

During this period, the North Bucks Association of

---

[56] *Op.cit.* n 2
[57] *Op.cit.* n 4

Independent Churches and Ministers was founded in 1818, and in 1819 the churches of Towcester and Potterspury joined the Association.[58] The church at Potterspury was represented on the committee by the Revd Gardner and Richard Scrivener. The report of the meeting of the Association in 1820, at which the Revd Gardner was not present, said that "he had been disabled for some months by infirmities, his pulpit being supplied by students of the Newport Pagnell Evangelical Institution". It also reported that the officiating minister preached once a fortnight at Yardley Gobion. The number of members at Potterspury was said to be 18 with 86 children in the Sunday School. By 1821 the membership had increased to 21, possibly due to the efforts of the students from Newport one of whom was probably James Slye who was later to become the pastor and to remain at Potterspury for over fifty years. Isaac Gardner died on 21 October 1821, and the Association report of 1822 says, "The last year has terminated the weakness and sufferings of the Revd. Isaac Gardner. He endured a long affliction with great patience". The first entry in *The Register of Funerals at Potterspury Chapple* [sic], kept by the sexton, states that "The Reverant Issac [sic] Gardner died Oct 21. 1821. Aged 67 years. Interred in Chapple [sic]".[59]

His memorial tablet in the Chapel bears these words:

> Let Gabriel take the Golden Harp and strike the trembling lyre;
> However high his strains shall rise, my notes shall still be higher.

In the 1980s, a group of visiting ministers were in the chapel and noticed that in one area the floor appeared to be rotten. They prodded the floorboards, which gave way, and to their dismay they found themselves looking down at what proved to be the remains of Isaac Gardner!

---

[58] Dr Williams' Library: *Proceedings and Reports of the North Bucks Association of Independent Churches and Ministers 1820-1829*
[59] NRO: *The Register of Burials of the Congregation of Protestant Dissenters Meeting in Potterspury in the County of Northampton 1821-1936*

James Slye and the Victorian Chapel: 1825-1873

The North Bucks Association supplied preachers to, reportedly, well-attended meetings at Yardley Gobion and the students of the Newport Academy supported the church at Potterspury until 1823 when one of them, James Slye, was invited to become the pastor. At the North Bucks Association meeting in 1823, which must have been the first he attended with Deacon Thomas Warr, he helped to conduct the devotional exercises. The meeting noted his arrival at Potterspury and were of the opinion that "He had a pleasing prospect of usefulness". The secretary of the Association received a letter from a member of the Church at Potterspury, but unfortunately does not say who, which said, "We confidently hope that the presence of so worthy a minister among us, will stimulate us to exert ourselves in a manner worthy of creatures who are born for eternity", which would seem to indicate that Slye was already well known to them. In his first year, a society was formed at Potterspury for visiting and relieving the sick of whatever denomination. Admirable though the Society's objectives were, they showed that they had an ulterior motive too, when they stated that "the visiting would afford an opportunity for pious persons to press the importance of divine truth on the mind of many, who in health, had been inattentive to the means of grace".

James Slye was ordained in June 1825 (the year his wife was admitted as a member), and for fifty years, until his resignation on 21 December 1873, offered in himself a remarkable example of an influential village ministry. During part of this time the vicar of the established church, John Hellins,[60] was of the opinion that the Independents were in open opposition to the village school, which he had started in 1817 with the help of the 4th Duke of Grafton[61] and The National Society, when he wrote in a letter to the Society that "… our school still continues notwithstanding the secret undermining and the open opposition which we experience from our good neighbours the sectaries of this parish, who call themselves Independents … The Dissenters of this place instruct their boys and girls on Sunday in their Meeting-House".[62] The Independents' attitude is not really surprising when one considers that the full title of the National Society was The National Society for Educating the Poor in the Principles of the Established Church. This interdenominational bickering prevented any state aid to education until 1833.[63]

Just one year into Slye's ministry the number of children in the Sunday school had increased from 36 to 106. A year later, in 1824, the number had increased to 140 and two new galleries were erected in the church to accommodate the increased congregation and Sunday school. The number of children remained at this figure until 1828 when they dropped to 100 due, it was reported, to the opening of a Sunday school by the Established Church. John Hellins first mentions this as a school for girls in 1825, when writing to the National Society, which he says was set up by his wife and two of the Duke of Grafton's daughters, Ladies Laura and Isobella Fitzroy, and that they taught the Church Catechism and reading and writing. Obviously this school had

Revd James Slye

60 The Revd John Hellins, BD, FRS. (See also *Northamptonshire Past & Present*, 1992/3 pp275-285)

61 George Henry Fitzroy,4th Duke of Grafton (1760-1844)

62 NRO: The Revd John Hellins, BD, FRS. Letters to the National Society, Northampton, 1817-1824

63 Michael Reed (1983) *The Georgian Triumph 1700-1830*

continued after Hellins's death in 1827 and may have then included boys.

In 1846 the Dissenters built their own school room adjoining the Chapel.

Table 1: Children in Independent Sunday school, Potterspury, 1820-1829[64]

1820	1821	1822	1823	1824	1825	1826	1827	1828	1829
86	86	86	106	140	140	140	140	100	95

By 1825 the suggestion was made that quite a few village people knew little of the Holy Scriptures and so the bold decision was made to enquire at every household to determine whether this was the true situation. The enquiry confirmed their suspicions that both at Potterspury and Yardley Gobion there were many people who were ignorant of the "Word of Life". Ebenezer White had arrived at a similar opinion, albeit of his own flock, twenty-five years earlier [q.v.]. In answer to this problem, many copies of the Bible were distributed by the Ladies' Association which had been formed to carry out this task. Another relevant but not at all surprising fact brought out by the enquiry was that many of the poor could not read. In an effort to help remedy this sorry state of affairs, another initiative was introduced and a school for adults was started. No mention is made of the efficacy of this enterprise, but after just two years a sewing-school was established in its stead! Yet another society was formed in 1828; this time a missionary society. In the same year Slye took on the added responsibility of preaching at Alderton, Northamptonshire.

In 1824 the North Bucks Association made the offer of a small sum to the church congregation at Potterspury on condition that they exerted themselves towards building a chapel at Yardley Gobion, to replace the room used for

---

[64] Data taken from Proceedings and Reports of the North Bucks Association of Independent Churches and Ministers

meetings which was proving too small for the increased audience. The fact that there was no parish church there may partly explain this anxiety to build a chapel there and so get in first. In fact, an established church, dedicated to St. Leonard, was not built there until 1864 although Bridges states "in Yardley Gobion there was a chapel dedicated to St. Leonard which had since become a public house".[65] Slye reported to the Association in 1826 that £20 and a piece of land had been obtained and so they granted £10 towards the total expected cost of £260. By the 19 April of the same year the chapel was built and opened although surprisingly no mention of this fact is made in the *Meeting Minute Book* but a brief footnote in a book of records says, "Yardley Chapel opened 1826. Cost £368.4s.10d". No further details are given. A tablet on the building is inscribed "Yardley Chapel 1826". At its completion, £25 was still owed to the builder but it was expected to soon clear the debt. The building was vested in trust entirely under the government of the pastor and church at Potterspury. By 1870 it had become very neglected and so it was restored, with Joseph Masom, Thomas Scrivener and John Foddy being the prime movers. William Kendall of Potterspury Lodge was the first subscriber towards the expense and the Duke of Grafton also subscribed. George Weston, the Duke's carpenter, made the new seats, and the gallery and organ were a gift from John Masom.

On 1 November 1828, James Slye carried out the burial of John Holloway of Yardley Gobion, the first to be interred in the new Burying Ground which had been laid out in part of a field adjacent to the chapel at Potterspury. James Langworth Slye, the Pastor's eight year old son, was interred there in 1837 so joining the many other young children, some as young as a few days or even hours, who were interred there at this period. The *Burial Register*[56] gives a clear indication of the alarming size of the infant mortality rate at that time and the number of young

65 NRS: J Bridges (1791) *History and Antiquities of Northamptonshire*
66 *Op.cit.* n 54

mothers who also died.

The name "Slye of Potterspury" became well known in non-conformist circles outside Potterspury mainly because of his authorship and publications, and, according to John Taylor,[67] in the summer months he ministered for many years at the Revd Rowland Hill's Surrey Chapel in the Blackfriars Road, London, whilst Hill made excursions to the provinces where his preaching is said to have attracted immense crowds. The first of Slye's books, *A Brief Narrative of the Rise and Progress of the Independent Church at Potterspury*, was published in 1831 and printed by H Dixon, a Stony Stratford bookseller. His other works, published in London, were: *Sermons on various Subjects* (1836); *The Investigator: or, an Inquiry into the Nature, Origin, and Scriptural Support of the Doctrine of the Personal Reign of Christ, etc.* (1843); *A Denominational Catechism for the Use of Dissenters of the Congregational or Independent Order* (1846); *The Old Mine Explored* (1850); *Home exercises for Spiritual Improvement* (1857); *A Guide to the use of the Scripture Promises* (1862).

Yardley Gobion Chapel with modern front

The *Northampton Mercury* of 12 April 1873 reported that to mark Slye's half-century at Potterspury the members of the church made presentations to him and Mary, his wife. First a capital tea was provided and then all assembled in the church where, after singing and prayers, many fine addresses were made by fellow nonconformists from near and far including Mr Gardner the son of Mr Slye's predecessor. Mr French from Buckingham praised James Slye's "exceedingly good preaching from the first", an attribute considered to be of paramount importance in a nonconformist pastor. Mr Westley of Blisworth ended his address by saying, "It was a grand thing for a minister of religion to maintain an unsullied character for fifty

---

[67] John Taylor (1891) *Old Nonconformist Memories, Potterspury*

years". This remark was followed by applause! The Revd Mr Lankaster of Newport Pagnell also referred to Mr Slye as a preacher and said, "The very fact of his preaching four or five thousand sermons, effectively and instructively, without repeating himself, was proof that he was a diligent student, and that he had what most ministers wanted more of – a great deal of tact". Slye was presented with a purse of eighty guineas and Mrs Slye with a handsome timepiece. This obviously joyful occasion ended with the singing of the hymn, *Abide with me.*

For some unexplained reason Slye made no entries in the *Church Meeting Minute Book* for the last seven years of his ministry which is surprising for one who was well known for his writings. Perhaps he had become ill, but no mention is made of this although he died a little over a year after his retirement. In fact no entries were made until 1875 when William Attwell, who succeeded Slye as pastor, wrote in the Minute Book that it was handed to him by Slye in 1875 and that the last entry is dated 30 December 1866.[68]

Before his resignation, he and his wife, daughter Eleanor and son Thomas (whose name was removed from the Roll of Members in 1878 for non-attendance) had left the Manse and, according to the 1871 census, were living in the High Street near to the dwelling of the village Headmaster, Job Wright.

He performed his last baptism on 6 August 1874 and his last burial on 27 August in the same year. During his time at Potterspury, 135 new members were admitted to the congregation and he carried out 558 baptisms. He died on 4 January 1876. A monumental inscription in the Chapel records the fact that James Slye passed away in 1876 and was interred in the family vault at Seal in Kent. Mrs Slye died in May 1880.

---

[68] *Op.cit.* n 2

The late Victorian, Edwardian & Georgian chapel: 1875-1920

After the Revd James Slye resigned the pastorate of the church, the pulpit was supplied by the students of Hackney College until Mr William Attwell, recently returned from Madagascar and living at Fulbourn in Cambridgeshire, accepted an invitation from the church to labour among them as pastor. He commenced his labours on Sunday, 20 June 1875. The Pastor soon set about reorganising church services in the two chapels but it was suggested by some members that his proposed alterations, if carried out, would probably lead to separation of the chapels at Potterspury and Yardley Gobion. Mr Attwell refused to let the matter be decided by a vote of the members and agreed that the services should be carried out as before. Discussion also took place on the material condition of the Potterspury Chapel and it was concluded that extensive alterations and improvements were needed. In true British fashion a committee was formed to ascertain the best course to adopt and to see that the work was carried out. Of course the first objective was to raise the necessary money to effect the alterations without delay. A Public Meeting, to discuss various proposals made by the committee, was to be held but before it could be called the Revd Attwell submitted his resignation, possibly, one suspects, as a result of the difference of opinion between the Potterspury and Yardley churches. Another Public Meeting, held to discuss the new situation, refused to accept his resignation. Mr Attwell explained that he was not happy with the relationship between Potterspury and the Yardley Chapel. A further meeting was called and the Pastor submitted to the meeting a set of fifteen rules for the guidance of the church, the congregation, and both chapels, as well as the Sunday Schools. Probably the most important of these rules were numbers one and two which stated that the Chapel at Yardley be regarded simply as a branch of the Pury church and congregation, and that the congregations of both chapels be considered as one congregation only, and that consequently there be but one church and that the Church be called the Potterspury & Yardley Gobion Congregational Church. Other important rules were included for the regulation of the financial arrangements of the church. He let it be understood that if all these rules and arrangements were enforced and carried out he would withdraw his resignation. Presumably his propositions were accepted because he did withdraw his resignation and continued as pastor, although the fact is not recorded in the *Meeting Minute Book.*

The Public Meeting to consider the state of the chapel at Potterspury was finally held on 27 January 1876 when the plans made by Mr Ingall of Birmingham for its restoration and improvements were considered and agreed. By July 1876 the work had been completed by Mr Pacey of Stony Stratford and the chapel was re-opened for public worship. One doorway was closed off and replaced by a new window and most of the existing windows were reglazed with a "more modern design" so replacing the original antique leaden casements, an example of which, until recently, could still be seen in the upper storey of the school room. Various other improvements were made including the provision of oil-lamps to replace the candles which, up to the time of the alterations, were used for lighting. The pulpit which Harrison had brought with him and had been used since those early days was retained and incorporated on a new platform which had been erected at the east end of the chapel instead of at the north side as previously. A 17th century oak chair with panelled back carved in low relief and with arms with turned supports remains on the platform. Could this chair possibly be the one in which John Heywood sat and preached when he could no longer ascend the pulpit because of declining health and had to be carried into the church and placed in his chair in one of the aisles?

In August the Revd Attwell resigned again and moved to Therfield, Herts in the following January. It became known that The Revd James Ault intended leaving Paulerspury so he was invited to occupy the pulpit at Potterspury. He accepted the invitation and commenced his pastorate in March 1877. At this point it seems worth noting the method used by Congregational churches to select their pastors. The candidate would be invited to preach on two or three occasions and if approved of by the deacons and subscribers (and sometimes the whole congregation) he would be invited to become the pastor. The pastor's ability as a preacher was of paramount importance. At the same time the candidate also had the opportunity to make his own assessment of the meeting before considering, with the help of prayer, whether to accept or reject the invitation. Other important decisions were also made in a like manner by the members meeting together. It is the doctrine of democracy applied to the church. The church members themselves then had the task of raising sufficient money for the maintenance of their minister and the upkeep of the chapel at Potterspury and from 1826 the Yardley Gobion chapel as well.

James Ault resigned in 1879 to be followed as pastor by David Griffiths who remained until 1881 when he too resigned. Henry Moulson, the next pastor, resigned after only two years, in 1883, and departed to Sheffield. He returned to Potterspury in 1907 as guest speaker at the 217th anniversary service.[69] The church was without a pastor once again and so a meeting of the church members was held to discuss the best steps to be taken for supplying the pulpit and carrying on the work of the church. At this meeting it was decided to become connected with the New College Preaching Station Society and that students from the College be invited to supply the pulpit for the time being. During this period, baptisms were carried out by

[69] *Op.cit.* n 6

the Revd Arthur E Claxton and the Revd Algernon AJ Andrews. In 1885 at a General Meeting of the Church and Congregation it was agreed to invite Ebenezer Willie Honour to be their pastor and he accepted on the condition that the Church (which of course meant the members) raise £50 per annum towards his stipend and that this be added to any grant of between £20 and £30 from the North Bucks Association, together with the minister's house, garden, coach-house, stable, wash-house and so on. Sadly, Mr Honour's wife, Hannah, died in 1888 and by the next year he had resigned from his pastorate which had lasted just four years. During his time at Potterspury he introduced some changes in the way in which services were conducted, and admitted sixteen new members.

Following this period of constant change when the church was in a very low state, along came, from Middleton in Derbyshire, the Revd James White who was to bring stability to the church by remaining as its minister for 22 years. He was to see them into the twentieth century and into their third century as a Congregation of Protestant Dissenters (who in 1972 were to become the Potterspury and Yardley Gobion United Reformed Church).

On 4 August 1890 an address by the Revd T Gasquoine, of Northampton delivered at the Bicentenary Services to mark the establishment of the Independent Congregation at Potterspury in 1690 and the Recognition Services of their new Pastor, the Revd James White, began with these words:

> No discerning Nonconformist could come accidentally upon the little ecclesiastical settlement of the Congregational Church of Potterspury and its surroundings without at once perceiving that he was on historic ground. As he looked on what our fathers would have called a faire meeting house and the comfortable manse adjoining ... he would be likely to say to himself, 'Here, I am sure, are the outward indications of a Church that has had no little influence in the past on the lives of villagers around it; and however outwardly it may be with the people who worship here now, whether they be

few or many, it is evident from the neatness and good appearance of all around that there are still those who love this place, and find it of their highest joy to contribute to its prosperity.

During his pastorate the church was very active as evidenced by the minutes of those days. He revived the Sunday School, the Band of Hope, and temperance work. Interestingly, in view of Mr White's temperance work, in 1895 one of the thirteen persons appointed as the Trustees of the Meeting House at Yardley Gobion was Thomas Pratt of Potterspury who was said to be a Beer Dealer! However, Kelly's Directory[70] says he was also a bootmaker. In addition to his pastoral duties, White was a member of the Board of Guardians and became a Parish Councillor in 1894 when he was elected with 140 votes. At the same election he also became a District Councillor and remained a very active member of both bodies for over fifteen years. At a meeting of the Parish Council on 23 July 1895 he forwarded a motion that the Council should consider the advisability of lighting the village during the winter months.[71] He was not, however, successful in convincing them of the need and it was many more years before anything was done about street lighting. Not dismayed, he immediately, together with two other councillors, began an enquiry into the water supply of the village following serious outbreaks of typhoid fever; but not until 22 years later, in 1917, did the village have mains water!

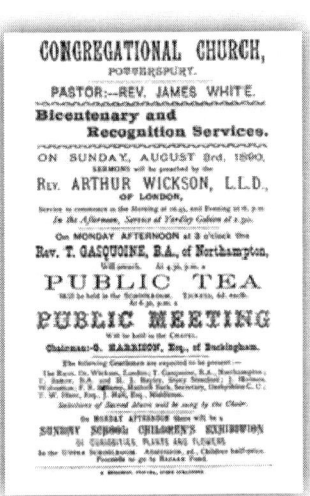

In 1904, possibly influenced by the publication by Charles

---

70 NRO: Kelly & Co, *Kelly's Directry of Northamptonshire* 1885
71 NRO: *Potterspury Parish Council Minute Book 1894*

Booth of his voluminous social survey, *Life and Labour of the People in London* which highlighted, among other things, the distress of the unemployed, White saw it as his duty to speak to the members about this subject and to suggest that they should raise, by means of a concert, funds to be sent to the County Fund for the Unemployed. It was agreed that the concert should take place on Christmas Day.[72]

By 1903, relations between the church and the village school had improved to such an extent that White became the Parish Council representative on the School Managers and also the District Education Sub Committee.[73] He often visited the school and signed the Log Book after having inspected the attendance registers.[74]

In 1911 he presented his resignation to the Church which was accepted with deep regret but coupled with sincere thanks for his long and faithful service, loving sympathy and help to the members in their everyday life.[75] The Parish Council also expressed regret at losing him and passed a vote of thanks for long and regular service.[76] An article in *The Northampton Mercury* under the heading *A Long Village Pastorate* says, "Mr. White, although sturdy in his Nonconformity and pronounced in his Liberalism, had always shown a broad and charitable spirit to all who differed from him, either politically or

James White & Wife

---

[72] *Op.cit.* n 63
[73] *Op.cit.* n 65
[74] NRO: Log Book: *Potterspury National School*
[75] *Op.cit.* n 63
[76] *Op.cit.* n 65

ecclesiastically, with the result that he had always been on the most friendly terms with the Vicar, the Revd. Walter Plant (another ardent temperance worker), and members of the Anglican Church; all uniting for the best interests of the parish at large". He was also said to have been honoured with the friendship of the Duke of Grafton,[77] "whose kindness and sympathy had been a stimulus to Mr. White in his ministry". The North Bucks Congregational Union also lost their honorary secretary when, in March 1912 he, together with his family, retired to Silloth, now in Cumbria on the Solway Firth, where he died in 1918.

The next Pastor was Revd W Angel who remained until 1924.

It seems appropriate at this time of remembering what has passed when at the same time looking forward to the future, to close with John Heywood's humble prayer at the end of his address on "Regeneration":

"God grant that of Pury it may be said at the Great Day,
That many Souls were born here."
Psalm lxxxvii,6

James White by Chapel

[77] Augustus Charles Lennox Fitzroy, 7th Duke of Grafton KG (1821-1918)

Appendix A

THE CHURCH COVENANTS

The following covenant is written down as the first entry in the Minute Book, dated 1740.

John Heywood's Covenant

WE THE PASTOR and Deacons and Members of the Church of Christ amen the Protestant Dissenters at Potter's-Pury in the County of Northampton do avouch the Lord this Day to be our God and ourselves to be his People in Truth and Sincerity of our Hearts and it is our Duty to give to Everyone a Reason of the Hope that is in us and since we live in a sad Day of Apostasy from the Glory of the Dear Redeemer & the Truths of the Gospel we therefore in the most solemn Manner express our Zeal for the Fundamentals of the Gospel. We most solemnly believe the Doctrine of the Holy Trinity the Supreme Godhead & true Divinity of the Son & Holy Spirit.

Revd Angel and Deacons

W E BELIEVE THE Doctrine of the mournful consequences of the Fall that we are born spiritually blind
& spiritually dead, that the whole Human Nature is
deprav'd ruin'd and lost which Corruption is commonly called
Original Sin.

W E BELIEVE THAT Christ's People are a People given
to Christ & chosen in Christ before the Foundation
of the World that Christ may have all the Glory of
their Salvation.

W E BELIEVE THE Doctrine of Justification by the im-
puted Righteousness of Christ alone and we are
pardn'd accepted & justify'd thro the Righteousness
received by Faith alone.

W E BELIEVE THE Doctrine of the Influence of his Holy
Spirit that Dear Redeemer will bring his children
home by a work of conversion by enlightening of
their minds with the Saving Knowledge of Christ renewing of
their wills & calling them to embrace Jesus Christ freely offered
in the Gospel.

W E BELIEVE THE Perseverance of all the Saints that
Christ will bring all his children safe home to Glory.

W E CALL HEAVEN & Earth Angels and Men to wit-
ness this Day that we recognize our Baptismal
Covenant & give up our selves to God the Father,
Son, & Spirit as our Creator Redeemer & Sanctifier in an
Everlasting Covenant never to be forgotten.

W E DO BIND our Selves to the Presence of God to
walk together in his ways to attend upon his Word,
Ordinances of Grace.

W E DO SINCERELY promise thro' divine assistance to
make the Glory of God without End, to watch
against Every Thing that wou'd offend God grieve

his Holy Spirit & bring reproach upon the good Ways of God & endeavour to adorn the Doctrine of God our Saviour in All Things to honor that high & holy name whereby we are called & to behave with that Strictness, Seriousness and Piety as becomes the Disciples of the Dear Redeeming Jesus.

W E DO SOLEMNLY promise to walk with all our Fellow Christians with all Humility, Tenderness & Love as Christ has loved us & given himself for us to avoid Jealousness Backslidings Suspicions & Censuring and Provoking secret Risings of Spirit to bear, forbear as Christ Has taught us and at all Times to watch against Every Thing that would justly offend our Fellow Christians and promise to submit to the Counsel & Advice of our Minister & Fellow Christians.

W E PROMISE TO behave with all possible Loyalty & allegiance to his Sacred Majesty King George to pray for him & all his Royal Family that God may bless them all & confound all the Designs of their Enemies both at home & abroad.

W E PROMISE TO cultivate the Duties of the Closet and Family that God may bless us & dwell with us: to abound in the Sanctification of the Lord's Day, diligently to attend upon the Means of Grace and to bring all we can under the Droppings of the Sanctuary.

A ND ALL THIS we promise not in our own Power & Strength but in the Name and Strength of our Lord Jesus Christ to whom with the Father & Holy Spirit be Everlasting Praises. Amen.

The following covenant is written down on a separate piece of paper and is not affixed in the Minute Book.

W E VOUCH THE Lord this Day to be our God and our Selves to be his People in the Truth and Sincerity of our Hearts.

W E CALL HEAVEN and Earth Angels and men to witness this Day that we recognise our Baptismal Covenant and give up our Selves to God the Father Son and Spirit as our Creator Redeemer and Sanctifier in everlasting Covenant never to be forgotten.

W E DO SINCERELY promise thro' divine assistant to make the Glory of God our Aim and End to watch against Every Thing that would offend God grieve his Holy Spirit and bring reproach upon the good ways of God and endeavour to adorn the Doctrines of God our Saviour in all things to honour that High and holy name whereby we are called and to behave with that Seriousness Strictness and Piety which becomes the Disciples of the dear Redeeming Jesus.

W E SOLEMNLY PROMISE to walk with all our Fellow Christians with all humility and Tenderness to love one another even as Christ has loved us and given himself for to avoid Jealousness Suspicions Backbitings Censurings Provokings secret Rising of Spirits then bear and forbear to give and to forgive as our dear Lord has taught us.

A T ALL TIMES we desire by the Help of divine Grace to watch against every Thing that would offend our fellow Christians and promise to be willing to submit to the advice and Counsel of our Minister and our Fellow Christians.

W E PROMISE TO behave with all possible loyalty and allegiance to his Sacred Majesty King George and to pray for him and all his Royal Family & that God may bless them and confound at the designs and blast the Counsels of all his Enemies both at Home and Abroad.

WE PROMISE TO behave cultivate the Duties of the Closet and promote Family Prayer that God may dwell with us and bless us and all that are dear to us. We also promise to abound in a strict sanctification of the Lord's Day and to bring all we can under the Dropping of God's Sanctuary. And all this we promise not in our own Strength and Power but in the name and Strength of our Lord Jesus Christ with whose Blood we desire this Covenant may be sprinkled.

An abridgement of the Church Covenant made by the Revd. Ebenezer White, a Candidate (1798-1800).

W E DO THIS Day solemnly avouch the Lord to be our God, and ourselves to be his People in the Truth & Sincerity of our Hearts. We call Heaven & Earth, Angels & Men to witness that this day we recognise our baptismal Covenant, and give up ourselves to God the Father Son & Spirit as our Creator, Redeemer, & Sanctifier, in an Everlasting Covenant never to be forgotten.

R ELYING UPON THE Lord Jesus Christ alone for Pardon and Salvation, we resolve with his Divine assistance, to make his Glory our Aim & End, to walk together in his ways, to attend upon his ordinances, to endeavour to adorn the Doctrines of God our Saviour in all things, to honour that High & Holy Name whereby we are called, and to behave with that Seriousness Strictness & Piety which becomes the Disciples of the dear Redeeming Jesus.

W E SOLEMNLY ENGAGE to walk with our Fellow Christians, with all Humility Tenderness & Love, with lowliness of Mind to submit to the advice & Counsel of each other, and to watch against Jealousies, Suspicions, Backbitings, Censurings, Provokings, & secret risings of Spirit, both to bear & forbear to give & forgive as our dear Lord hath taught us.

W E CONSIDER OURSELVES under renewed obligations to cultivate the Sacred Exercises of Private & Social Prayer -- to maintain the stated worship of God in our Families, to Sanctify his holy Sabbath and to use our influence for bringing others under the droppings of his Sanctuary & Power, but in the Name of Strength of our Lord Jesus Christ, with whose Blood we earnestly desire this our Covenant may be sprinkled -- Amen

The following Covenant is contained in the Revd. James Slye's history of the Independent Church at Potterspury, 1831, and is said, by him, to have been drawn up by Mr. Heywood.

1. We avouch the Lord this day to be our God, and ourselves to be his people, in the truth and sincerity of our hearts.

2. We call heaven and earth, angels and men to witness this day, that we recognise our Baptismal Covenant, and give ourselves to God the Father, Son, and Spirit, as our Creator, Redeemer, and Sanctifier, in an everlasting Covenant never to be forgotten.

3. We do bind ourselves in the presence of God to walk together in his ways, to attend upon his word and ordinances of his grace, resolving to cleave to the Lord Jesus Christ, and to him alone, for pardon and salvation.

4. We do sincerely promise, through divine assistance, to make the glory of God our aim and end, to watch against every thing that would offend God, grieve his holy Spirit, and bring a reproach upon the good ways of God.

5. We solemnly promise to walk with all our fellow-Christians with all humility and tenderness; to love one another, even as Christ has loved us and given himself to us; to avoid jealousies, suspicions, backbitings, censurings, provokings, secret risings of spirit against them; to bear and forbear, to give and forgive,, as our dear Lord has taught us.

6. At all times we desire, by the help of divine grace, to watch against any thing that would offend our fellow-Christians; and promise to be willing to submit to the advice and counsel of our Minister and fellow-Christians.

7. We promise to behave with all possible loyalty and allegiance to his sacred Majesty King George, and pray for him and all his Royal Family, that God may bless them, confound all the designs and blast the counsels of all enemies both at home and broad.

8. We promise to cultivate the duties of the Closet and to promote family prayer, that God may dwell with us and

bless us, and all that are dear to us. We also promise to abound in the strict sanctification of the Lord's day, and to bring all we can under the droppings of God's sanctuary. And all this we promise, not in our own strength and power but in the name and strength of our Lord Jesus Christ, with whose blood we desire this Covenant may be sprinkled.

Appendix B

1658 *Pedder's Farm*, Potterspury, purchased by Edward Scrivener, later passing to his two daughters and ultimately to Richard Scrivener.

1660 Restoration of Charles II.

1661 *The Corporation Act.*

1662 *The Act of Uniformity.*
Revd Joseph Newel (or Nevill), vicar of the Established Church at Potterspury, is ejected but later conforms.

1664 *The Conventicle Act*, forbidding all religious meetings but those of the Anglican Church.

1665 *The Five Mile Act*, forbidding nonconforming ministers to teach in schools or live within five miles of a corporate town.

1669 Report on dissenters and conventicles instigated by Archbishop Sheldon.

1670 Report to Bishop of Peterborough by Archdeacon John Palmer of Northampton.

1672 *Declaration of Indulgence*, (suspending laws against nonconformists).

1673 Cancellation of *Declaration Indulgence* and passing of *The Test Act* making all holding office under the Crown to:
(1) take the Sacrament according to the Anglican rite, and
(2) make a declaration against transubstantiation.

1685 Death of Charles II.
Accession of James II.

1687 *Declaration of Indulgence*, suspending all laws against Roman Catholics and dissenters.

1688 *2nd Declaration of Indulgence.* (ordered to be read in churches).
James II flees to France. (23rd December)

1689 Accession of William and Mary.
The Toleration Act, affording some relief to Protestant nonconformists.

1690	**Revd Michael Harrison, ejected minister, arrives in Potterspury to form an Independent congregation in barn of *Pedder's Farm.***
1691	**Revd Michael Harrison purchases *Pedder's Farm* from Richard Scrivener for £70.**
1694	Death of Queen Mary. Harrison publishes a paper supporting child baptism.
1700	Michael Harrison publishes *Twelve Divine Hymns: Composed for the Lord's Table, and the Lord's Day.*
1701	Death of James II. Louis XIV acknowledges the Pretender, James Edward Stuart, as King of England.
1702	Death of William III. Accession of Queen Anne. Declaration of War against France.
1704	Queen Anne's Bounty instituted, by which the first-fruits of benefices are set aside for the benefit of the poorer clergy. Battle of Blenheim.
1706	**Revd Michael Harrison leaves Potterspury for St. Ives, Cambs.**
1707	Union of England and Scotland.
1709	**Revd Michael Harrison sells *Pedder's Farm* to John Gough of Highgate.**
1709	**Revd Mr Bennett arrives and stays for short time and is followed by Revd Isaac Robinson who becomes pastor.**
1713	The Peace of Utrecht. Acknowledgement by France of the Protestant succession in Great Britain.
1714	*The Schism Act* passed, forbidding anyone not a member of the Church of England to keep a school.
1714	Death of Queen Anne. Accession of George I. **Revd William Bushnell, pastor. Congregation obtains 21 year lease on chapel and house.**
1719	Repeal of the *Schism Act.*
1727	Death of George I. Accession of George II.
1729	Philip Doddridge sets up a Dissenting Academy at Market Harborough which transfers, with him, to Northampton at the end of the year.
1732	**Congregation purchases chapel and house and appoints trustees.**

1735   Revd Samuel Tailor, pastor.

1739   Rise of Methodists.
Revd John Heywood, from Lincoln, becomes pastor of the Independent church.

1740   John Heywood's ordination. His *Hymns or Spiritual Songs, Chiefly taken from the Holy Scriptures* published in London, and dedicated "To the Reverend Philip Doddridge, D.D."

1746   Battle of Culloden: defeat of the Old Pretender and suppression of the rebellion by the Duke of Cumberland ("The Butcher"). **John Heywood notes in Meeting Minute Book, "General Thanksgiving for the defeat of the Rebels."**

1760   Death of George II
Accession of George III.

1760   **John Heywood goes to London to join in address of congratulation to the new king.**

1768   **Mrs Heywood admitted as church member.**

1775   American War of Independence.

1778   **Death of John Heywood.**

1780   **Chapel and Manse erected.**

1782   **Revd John Goode, ordained pastor.**

1783   United States independence acknowledged by England.

1794   **Revd John Goode removes to the Independent Church of Christ, White Row, London. Church members from Towcester leave, and set up separate church there.**
Revd George Vowell (candidate). Dies same year.
Revd Stephen Morrell (candidate). Removes to Kilsby.

1795   **Revd William Whitefoot (candidate). Removes to Hanslope taking members from Hanslope with him.**
Revd John Savage (candidate). Removes to Farnham.

1796   **Revd John May (candidate). Removes 1797.**

1797   **Revd William Saunders (candidate). Removes.**

1798   **Revd Ebenezer White (candidate). Removes to Hertford.**

1800   Act of Union between Great Britain and Ireland.

1805   **Revd Isaac Gardner, pastor.**

1811   Prince of Wales made Regent because of king's alleged insanity.

1814   **Mr Smith bequeaths the sum of £100 to the Independent cause at Potterspury.**

1817   National School for boys opened in Potterspury.

1818   Revd Isaac Gardner resigns.
North Bucks Association of Independent Churches & Ministers founded.

1819   Church joins North Bucks Association.

1820   Death of George III.
Accession of Regent as George IV.

1821   Revd Gardner dies and is interred in Chapel.

1823   Revd James Slye, pastor.

1825   Revd James Slye is ordained.

1826   Chapel built at Yardley Gobion, at cost of £368.

1828   John Holloway, from Yardley Gobion, first person interred in new Burying Ground, adjacent to Potterspury chapel.

1829   Catholic Emancipation Act.

1830   Death of George IV.
Accession of William IV.

1831   Publication of James Slye's *Brief Narrative of the Rise and Progress of the Independent Church at Potterspury.*
Independent churches join together to form Congregational Union.

1836   James Slye publishes *Sermons on various Subjects.*

1837   Death of William IV.
Accession of Queen Victoria.
Church registered for the Solemnization of Marriage.

1843   James Slye publishes *The Investigator: or, an Inquiry into the Nature, Origin, and Scriptural Support of the Doctrine of the Personal Reign of Christ etc.*

1846   Sunday school room built.
James Slye publishes *A Denominational Catechism for the Use of Dissenters of the Congregational or Independent Order.*

1850   James Slye publishes *The Old Mine Explored.*

1853   Thomas Coleman publishes *Memories of the Independent Churches in Northamptonshire.*

1857   James Slye publishes *Home Exercises for Spiritual Improvement.*
Girls school opened in Potterspury. (National)

1862   James Slye publishes *A Guide to the Use of the Scripture Promises.*

1870   The Elementary Education Act. (establishing school boards)
Infants school opened in Potterspury. (National)

1873 Church celebrates half-century of Revd Slye as pastor. Revd James Slye retires.

1874 Infant school opened in Yardley Gobion.

1875 Revd William Attwell, pastor.

1876 Chapel restored and altered.
Revd William Attwell removes to Therfield.
Education Act (making elementary education nearly compulsory).

1877 Revd James Ault, pastor.

1879 Revd Ault resigns.
Revd David Griffiths, pastor.

1881 Revd Griffiths removes to Wington.
Revd H Moulson, pastor.

1883 Revd Moulson resigns.

1883 Girl's school opened in Yardley Gobion.

1885 Revd EW Honour, pastor.

1886 Mrs Ann Scrivener leaves £40 legacy to church.

1889 Revd Honour resigns.

1890 Revd James White, pastor. Church celebrates bicentennial of foundation.

1894 First Potterspury Parish Council elected. Revd James White a member.

1903 Revd James White becomes the Parish Council representative on the School Managers and also the District Education Committee.

1904 Concert held on Christmas Day to raise money for the County Fund for the Unemployed.

1910 Mrs Sarah Iliffe bequeaths £50 to purchase a new organ for the chapel.

1911 Revd White resigns.

1912 Revd White departs for Silloth.
Revd W Angel, pastor.

Appendix C

SUCCESSION OF MINISTERS

1690 Revd Michael Harrison
(removed to St Ives 1706, died Jan 1726/7)   Pastor

1709 Revd W Bennett   Candidate

1709 Revd Isaac Robinson
(removed to Chesham, Bucks c.1711, died c.1732)   Pastor

1714 Revd William Bushnell
(removed to Andover 1729, died May 1744)   Pastor

1735 Revd Samuel Tailor
(removed to Long Melford, Suffolk)   Pastor

1739 Revd John Heywood
(died Potterspury, 1 January 1778)   Pastor

1782 Revd John Goode
(removed to London 1794)   Pastor

1794 Revd George Vowell
(died 1794)   Candidate

1794 Revd Stephen Morrrell
(removed to Kilsby 1794)   Candidate

1795 Revd William Whitefoot
(removed to Hanslope 1795)   Candidate

1795 Revd John Savage
(removed to Farnham 1795)   Candidate

1796 Revd John May
(removed 1797)   Candidate

1797 Revd William Saunders
(removed 1797)   Candidate

1798 Revd Ebenezer White
(removed to Hertford 1800)   Candidate

1805　Revd Isaac Gardner
(partly retired 1818, died Potterspury 1821)　　Pastor

1823　Revd James Slye
(retired 1873, died Potterspury 15 January 1876) Pastor

1875　Revd William Attwell
(removed to Therfield 1876)　　Pastor

1877　Revd James Ault
(resigned 1879)　　Pastor

1879　Revd David Griffiths
(removed to Wington 1881)　　Pastor

1881　Revd Henry Moulson
(removed to Sheffield 1883)　　Pastor

1885　Revd Ebenezer Willie Honour
(resigned 1889)　　Pastor

1890　Revd James White
(retired 1912, died Silloth 1918)　　Pastor

1912　Revd W Angel
(removed to Stony Stratford 1924)　　Pastor

Appendix D

TRUSTEES OF POTTERSPURY & YARDLEY GOBION CONGREGATIONAL CHURCH

1714

John Saywell	Luffield Abbey	yeoman
John Watts	Paulerspury	yeoman
John Wickens	Paulerspury	yeoman
Edward Gray	Paulerspury	yeoman
Thomas Foukes	Towcester	collermaker
Henry Rockingham	Potterspury	chandler
William Addington	Potterspury	chandler
Hugh Boswell	Yardley Gobion	

1732

John Saywell	Luffield Abbey	grazier
Richard Scrivener	Potterspury	yeoman
John Wicken	Paulerspury	yeoman
John Buncher	Potterspury	yeoman
Richard Brown	Yardley Gobion	yeoman
John Smith	Yardley Gobion	yeoman
Henry Brown	Stony Stratford	cordwainer
William Addington	Potterspury	flaxdresser
Edward Scrivener	Potterspury	flaxdresser
William Warr	Potterspury	cordwainer
John Hawley	Paulerspury	carpenter
William Hawley	Paulerspury	carpenter
Robert Howlett (younger)	Paulerspury	carpenter
John Bitcheno	Paulerspury	sneathmaker
John Bland	Yardley Gobion	carpenter
John Warr	Yardley Gobion	shoemaker

1776

John Bitcheno	Paulerspury	sneathmaker
John Smith	Yardley Gobion	yeoman

Joseph Scrivener	Potterspury	gent
(son of Richard Scrivener, yeoman)		
Joshua Wood	Potterspury	yeoman
Joseph Scrivener jnr	Potterspury	
Richard Scrivener jnr	Brownswood Green	grazier
John Bland	Potterspury	grocer
John Alexander	Potterspury	yeoman
William Robinson	Potterspury	labourer
William Brown	Yardley Gobion	yeoman
Thomas Wood	Moor End	yeoman
Richard Bland	Yardley Gobion	carpenter
Robert Woodward	Yardley Gobion	yeoman
Samuel Glinn	Yardley Gobion	blacksmith
Edward Risley	Yardley Gobion	tailor
Edward Capron snr	Paulerspury	yeoman
Edward Capron jun.	Paulerspury	yeoman
Richard Brown	Stony Stratford	cordwainer
William Hawley	Paulerspury	yeoman
Neal Newman	Paulerspury	yeoman
John Tite	Blakesley	yeoman
Richard Ashbourn	Yardley Gobion	butcher
Richard Brown	Yardley Gobion	yeoman
Thomas Butteriss	Shutlanger	weaver

1824

Richard Scrivener	Puxley	farmer
Richard Scrivener	Potterspury	farmer
Joseph Scrivener	Alderton	farmer
Eli Elkins	Linford, Bucks	farmer
John Warr	Potterspury	shoe mnftr
Joshua Wood	Potterspury	farmer
George Claridge	Puxley	gent
Richard Scrivener	Cosgrove	farmer
Joseph Scrivener	Potterspury	miller
William Tompkins	Wakefield Lodge	gent
Thomas Holman	Potterspury	timber dealer
William Brown	Yardley Gobion	mason
William Sanders	Yardley Gobion	draper

1881

Enoch Iliffe	Potterspury	farmer
Thomas Scrivener	Potterspury	

William Wilkins Sanders	Potterspury	
Thomas Warr	Yardley Gobion	coal merchant
Joseph Wood	Potterspury	farmer
Alfred Scrivener	Potterspury	miller
Job Scrivener	Potterspury	miller
Samuel Valentine	Potterspury	miller
Joseph Holloway	Potterspury	tailor
John Samuel Griffiths	Leicester	dispenser
Ladd Joseph Scrivener	Buckingham	printer
William White	Towcester	grocer
George Pacey	Stony Stratford	cabinet maker

1895

James White	Potterspury	Protestant dissenting minister
Albert Gray	Wakefield, Potterspury	Clerk of Works
William John Swain	Yardley Gobion	labourer
Thomas Warr	Yardley Gobion	coal merchant
Thomas Holloway	Yardley Gobion	miller
James Kightly	Yardley Gobion	shoemaker
George Weston	Yardley Gobion	carpenter
Job Scrivener	Potterspury	miller
George Osborne	Potterspury	wheelwright
John Wise	Potterspury	plasterer
Arthur Frank Meakins	Potterspury	painter
Thomas Pratt Snr	Potterspury	beer dealer

1902

Job Scrivener	Potterspury	miller
Alfred Scrivener	Potterspury	miller
James White	Potterspury	minister
Albert Gray	Wakefield, Potterspury	Clerk of Works
Arthur F Meakins	Potterspury	painter
Robert Leonard Hobson	Potterspury	builder
Edgar John Davis	Potterspury	butcher
William John Swain	Potterspury	labourer
Jeremiah Tapp		
Percy William Gray		
Henry Moulson	Potterspury	
Thomas Warr	Yardley Gobion	coal merchant

Appendix E

NAMES GIVEN AT BAPTISMS 1740-1856
(100 years)

Table 2: Number of Baptisms

	Fe-males	Males	Totals	mean per year
1740/49	53	58	111	11.1
1750/59	76	59	135	13.5
55/2	27	46	73	14.6
No records for 18 years!				
2683/134	23	37	60	7.5
1790/99	21	34	55	5.5
01/09/18 00	17	15	32	3.2
85451/8 97	25	35	60	6
1820/29	29	16	45	4.5
610/13	36	71	107	10.8
1840/49	84	79	163	16.3
13307/4 10	47	47	94	13.4
Totals	438	497	935	6.8

The Baptism Register dates from 1740 with an unexplained break of 18 years from 1764 until 1782.

The table 2 show the total number of baptisms, and tables 3 and 4 show the top 75% of female and 75% of male names chosen during a recorded period of one hundred years. There are no real surprises because these are also the most common names used generally during that period; with Mary heading the list of girls and John heading the list of boys. A glance at their parents' names shows a similar pattern. Until the mid-nineteenth century most were given only one name so only the first name has been used in compiling these tables. There is one Marmaduke and one Temperance.

Table 3: Female Names - most popular 75% of total (438)

Name	1740	1750	1760	1782	1790	1800	1810	1820	1830	1840	1850	Totals	% of all females
Mary	13	16	9	5	4	5	5	4	9	6	6	82	18.72
Elizabeth	6	9	5	2	4	0	3	3	5	10	7	54	12.33
Sarah	7	12	1	2	1	0	2	4	2	13	6	50	11.42
Ann/Anne	10	11	3	5	1	1	3	3	1	3	3	44	10.05
Eleanor	2	4	0	1	1	2	1	4	1	5	2	23	5.25
Jane	1	3	0	1	1	0	0	2	2	3	2	15	3.42
Hannah	5	1	3	1	1	1	0	0	0	1	0	13	2.97
Caroline	0	0	0	1	2	1	1	1	0	2	3	11	2.51
Emma	0	0	0	0	0	0	0	0	0	4	6	10	2.28
Maria	1	0	0	1	0	0	1	2	2	3	0	10	2.28
												312	71.23

Table 4: Male Names - most popular 75% of total (497)

Name	1740	1750	1760	1782	1790	1800	1810	1820	1830	1840	1850	To-tals	% of all males
John	15	17	10	8	5	2	7	4	7	10	4	89	17.91
William	9	16	8	4	8	3	2	2	11	9	7	79	15.9
Thomas	9	9	6	6	6	3	6	2	13	9	5	74	14.89
George	2	1	4	0	0	0	2	1	11	15	2	38	7.65
Joseph	0	1	3	3	1	1	4	1	2	11	5	32	6.44
Richard	4	5	3	2	3	1	4	0	2	3	2	29	5.84
James	3	4	2	2	1	1	1	0	1	2	2	19	3.82
Henry	2	2	1	1	0	0	0	1	3	0	2	12	2.41
												372	74.85

BIBLIOGRAPHICAL SOURCES

Other than those fully titled in the text

Josiah Bull 1864	Memorials of Revd Willam Bull, N[orthmptonshire] L[ibraries]
Thomas Coleman 1853	Memories of the Independent Churches in Northamptonshire
Revd. T. Gasquoine 1891	Old Northamptonshire Memories: Potterspury, NL
Revd. Asher Goldberg 1907	A Short History of the Parish of Potterspury-cum-Yardley
A. Gordon 1917	Freedom after Ejection, 1690-92
John Hibbs 1988	The Country Chapel
J. Hunter 1842	Life of Oliver Heywood, NL
T.S. James 1867	The History of the Litigation and Legislation respecting Presbyterian Chapels and Charities in England and Ireland between 1816 and 1849
J. Moore, Trans	Congregational Historical Society, IV & V
Roy Porter 1982	English Society in the Eighteenth Century
L.C.B. Seaman 1981	A New History of England
Charles Surman 1882	Biographical Index of Nonconformist Ministers
Walter Wilson	History and Antiquities of Dissenting Churches, III
W.T. Whitley 1916	A Baptist Bibliography

Printed in Great Britain
by Amazon